After This

After This

Marcus O'Donnell

Clouds of Magellan

© 2025. Copyright images and text Marcus O'Donnell

All rights reserved. No part of this publication may be reproduced without permission

Clouds of Magellan Press, Melbourne
www.cloudsofmagellanpress.net

ISBN: 978-0-6486361-7-5 (paperback)

Also available in hardback
ISBN: 978-0-6486361-6-8 (hardback)

Acknowledgments

'Ariel's cycle' was previously published in *Verandah*

Contents

One

    after this   11

Two

    blood's kisses   23
    weighted   31
    study for a portrait   33
    this possible sadness   34
    madlines   37

Three

    rain or tears named or not   45
    mutations   49
    air wet and beaded   51
    figure of dreams   52
    up all night   55
    veil of tears   57

Four

    art gallery Northampton Massachusetts   61
    getting ready   63
    on photographing black holes   64
    touch me not   67

Five

    Ariel's cycle   75

A strange appearance: note on images

To one on his back in the dark a voice tells of a past. With occasional allusions to the present and more rarely to a future as for example, You will end as you now are.

Samuel Beckett

What we call texts escape us as the dream escapes us on waking, or the dream evades us in dreams. We follow it, things go at top speed, and we are constantly – what a giddy and delicious sensation! – surprised. In the dream as in the text we go from one amazement to another. I imagine many texts are written completely differently, but I am only interested in texts that escape.

Hélène Cixous

One

after this

After these things, I saw a door standing open in heaven. The first voice that I had heard speaking to me like a trumpet said, "Come up here, and I will show you what must happen after this."

(Revelation 4:1)

i

apocalypse is a   banal magic
apparently   all eyes
but actually   a cacophony of signs

a lottery of cell division
a crack in the sky

         premonitions performed
         and materialised

                   in bodies

         the innards   of all divinations
         wet colour   masking
         hope's   musculature

                      sweating mystery
                      damp with death

ii

each organ has its   sentry daemon

the lung god whose hands rock bellows for breath
spleen's angel funnelling to excrete and ameliorate
Prometheus guards the liver having paid
for sharing the secret of fire with his own

but the pancreas   who guards that gland

                                who   regulates
                                this   regulator
                                of   sweetness
                                who   ghosts
                                its   lush flesh

we didn't know   but should have guessed
as we watched you enter   haloed with resolve
stick thin   that each of those sentries
inching forward   had stood down
propelled by something   other
let loosed   in you

we didn't know   but should have guessed

what would happen   after this
after   that day
the feast   the family

iii

when I went with you to the hospital the doctor kept referring to
your pictures by which he meant the malignancies that blotted
those odd electrical innerscapes
                                        that hung

                        lit beside him

                        perverse holy cards
                        sentry daemons
                        become monstrous

he asked if you had been having trouble with your memory

          half hearing him you said
                        looking over at us
                        your two boys

      I have plenty of wonderful memories

          half heard   but fully answered

I thought of your other pictures
that four weeks earlier
had cycled on repeat
at your 90th birthday

          a life   not just a body scanned

iv

in those days you didn't report any visions
of jasper and carnelian
or rainbows or emerald thrones
your mysticism more mundane

Babies   sons   cars   planes

leaving   and   coming home

you laughed about your dreams
hesitantly embracing their strangeness
realising in that quiet no-fuss way of yours
that something new was happening

that this was not the life   sharp with visible edges
                               that you had always lived

on your second day in hospital you began to take your leave

                 dreaming of babies

I woke up and thought (*you said*) how am I going to feed the baby (*but you had not awoken*) and then I thought (*thinking against the logic of dreams*) I'm sure I only have two children, oh well I thought (*putting that puzzle aside*) I'll find something somehow (*pragmatic and resourceful even in dreams*) then I woke up (*half-awake now*) I thought who's looking after Marcus and Anthony while I'm here (*first thoughts*) then I realised where I was and that *you* were looking after *me*

                 fully awoken

you smiled
             unsure of dream navigation
             but comfortable enough
             with both life and death

at least I pulled myself back (*you said*) back here again (*not quite ready yet*)

the next day was about landings　　　　　　dreaming of flight

I was in a plane (*you said*) coming into land and I was wondering how will I get back here (*your world had settled* here *in this hospital bed*) I thought maybe Marcus will be there to meet me (*you had always met yourself looked after yourself back from your bus trips or even your longer miles now dreaming you looked to me*) anyway I got back (*you said*)

then two days before you died daily flight paths dissolved

in the early morning	*you said*
I drifted in and out of sleep	*amorphous time*
I thought	*you said*
will I get out of bed	*90 years of mornings*
get up	*ever harder*
shower	*scrubbed*
get in the car	*independent*
go to church	*devout*
or am I in that other place	*this unfamiliar here*
I opened my eyes	*you said*
oh I'm in that other place	*landed*
life reconfigured	you touched the ground
settled	and then you were gone

v

after the hospital visit my cousin asked about my beliefs

so you're a Buddhist
        you believe in reincarnation
                she says
                        leaving that last part
                                hanging quizzically

I didn't want to talk about it   in the car
                                        in this way

to pin the question of death   down   to

                                          comings
                                          and goings

but I wanted to honour   the candour

(where death had settled like a form of intimacy between us)

                not exactly
                      not literally
                                I began

what I should have said is   death is
a conversation we have   over days
then weeks   then years
you and I   have in us
many lives   none of them past
when you die   your absence is both
irrevocable   and present

what I should have said is   the living pass through
                                                the bardo not the dead

instead I said
        something about
                the interconnectedness of life

we are what we become   and all of it
the world a flow   between the limited
                               and the limitless

(my cousin didn't find abstraction helpful)

she needed to talk of   bodies and places
                                         spaces and time

   what I should have said is

we are   all the oceans heating up
the ice   melting
the extinct wolves   reintroduced into wild places

we are   salmon swimming upstream
the bears   that eat them
the scavenging birds   that spread
their nitrous remnants   across the earth

we are   the trees that grow air green
we each contain   multitudes
hide   bone deep malignancies

apocalypse   shines and dances

                       in our bodies

Two

blood's kisses

i

this
i have imagined
here
as earth

this
i have imagined
here
as flesh

these
points
plotted
to navigate

these
co-ordinates
mapped
to bear
easily
with strength

these boundaries
set to contain

these furrows
to check
all leakage

ii

this count
these lines
shaded dark
then muted grey
scour the intimacy
of my veins
purport
to show
a hidden
(un) known
reality

ruptured
the body's
innocent delight
that its shadow
lays behind
the trace
of its certainty
in light

iii

i draw the body
bone and curve
sinew and line
i note
the interlocking
order of its curvature
i circumnavigate
its edge
i cast a likeness

mutable   bent   angled

iii

i have kept count
of the breath
i have watched
the tip of the nose
and led the mind's
eye from the point
four finger widths
below the navel
to the point at
the tip of
the crown

the breath
an antidote
to fear
a prompt
a smile

no awakening

iv

then suddenly
as brush feathered
the edge of a yellow line
joy jumped
and woke
reverie

v

this is a
new dispensation
where flesh is
no longer redeemed
because no longer
held to ransom

the eschaton
is now

no waiting

in these end times
there are those who will
bear the mark of the lamb
and those who will bear
the mark of the beast

we

we bear the
mark of blood's kisses

weighted

The self is a sacrament
knotted skin-tight
the days stinging like bees

this fictitious skin
inked with an old tale
of endings, scared
and itchy, a type of
awe stretched over water.

Max Jacob said we have
eyes in our stomach
gut visions of
gods, flesh
ghosted and sensual

we are weighted to care
every decision's ghost
an unfurling anchor
that turns us
with awkward grace
towards another.

study for a portrait

I was an artist in the first dream
but spent the night writing out
a complex text in ancient English
carefully italicising words and
sentences to emphasise each point,
a monastic dedication to craft.

I was a detective in another,
an Irish night, three people
converging at the news of death,
don't worry about me I said
worry about her children,
a hasty distancing of grief.

All writing is rewriting
this poem one I have written before,
with its dream codes
its syntax of loss
its clustering of anxieties
its unreachable daylight
its flickering eyes
its haze of rain
its absent children
its sudden but not
unexpected news of death.

Dreams are like a Francis Bacon painting
fragments of ecstasy spilled across a canvas
life death and air commingle
and desire
framed but edgeless
pools in milky grey marks
tight on painted skin.

this possible sadness

Is sadness just the memory of sadness
that first *irremediable moment,*
as Kristiva calls it, or is every sadness
an anticipation of what Celine called
the *greatest possible sorrow,*
an urgent passion that lets us become
fully ourselves before dying?

In sadness not in spite of it
we make and remake each other.

So how have I fashioned you
cut edges where secrets explode
made marks as equations of longing
and wet with cerulean blue ink
tattooed skin stretched between us?

How have you fashioned me
cut triangles as days
lit calendars with votive lamps
and threaded moss as gentleness
wherever absence rubbed against us?

You were telling me about your
grandmother's tears, then the rain began
and you paused to proclaim
the storm – we had been waiting for that
longing for that rain – the rain gods heard me
you said, tone and mood shifting to mock triumph.

Had the world suddenly in that moment
distilled your long dead grandmother's sorrow
watering the garden with her sacrifices
freshening the air with her silences
scenting your memory with the smell
of summer rain that comes fast but doesn't stay long?

I dream of a stranger in our blackened house
he leaves hooded in rain, night a pathway
rain the medium of his sadness in a
cinematic finale of dark wet light.

madlines

Identity is the product of loss.

Jacques Lacan

i

my eyes are blue
my hand concoctor
of secrets
my knees creak
my feet   feet that flee from scenes crime

desire's body
desire's mind   desire's heat

me

my body's ache
this body

             quivering

curved as   shadow
clinging round   flesh

we are memories

             of that which we
             have not known

             ripe with potentiality
             for   dis   ease

ii

I have known
here within these walled
vaulted veins
blood's fire

here nursed
desire for obliteration

that brotherly moment
of madness   two men's bodies

                                    locked closet of desire
                                    open and aired

                                    they say one to another

take   take this and eat
this   this is my body

take   take this and drink
this   this is my blood

I have imagined
the soft melting center
I have imagined
the belly's hard arm

I am love's poet
these sunset eyes my
rhymed syllables

what cannot be in
armoured flesh
has been and
I have survived
a chemical explosion
                            that reverses time

iii

        we have taken tongue
          and tied tide
           between us
              and
          this time we
          have let run
          the twisted
         hairs of bodies
          and tangle
          has become
     the arms and legs
            the
         eyes and ears
           the nose
           the teeth
            of our
          love making
            knotted
 in this wet sticky reality
             two
        soul enriched
         gland driven
          bone held
       blood breathed
        fleshed selves

          no bodies

         shimmering
            the
          madlines
             of
            our
           vitality

Three

rain or tears named or not

looking through
 rain or tears

each wet pulse
breathes itself loose
to trickle
 down

shattering into
microcosmic clones
dispersing into air

atomised mirrored
 worlds

at once crystalline
 and dirty

constant rain like constant tears
with slight touch
causes simultaneously
mark and erasure

 teaches concealment
 and disclosure

beyond the sheer curtain
of rain's immensity

seen briefly
 storm's eye

off with the mask
of frightened gods
who fear that
sight will stem desire
water air
earth fire

each   a filter
which tears away fear

smudged sightings
muddy visions
charred remnants
fluid forms

magnified or myopic
both crooked
ways of seeing

each   abstract
and   distinguish form

rain   and tears
yes   or no
named   or not

form is shadow

mutations

a flower   outside my window
                      in the flow of hours
                      not just days
changes   from white to pink
dies   in a muffled red
its   suddenly burnt edging

                      tinged with cruelty

I am astonished
at such   energetic mutation
but that   astonishment
cannot match
this plant's   strange and crisp
                      coded knowing

                                    and then

mist comes from below
                          rises into
                          late afternoon

no glue binds this
visible air
except its intent
                          to come
                          to drift
                          to cover

the mist signals
that darkness
                          another formless
                          name of air
will soon
shatter this   pretty softness

no climax   no plateau

air wet and beaded

rain

the watery world soul
the suddenly visible

starting   and stopping
interrupted   not ending
air cool   or warm
always   expectant

                    harboring rain

at all latitudes
not just the tropical
rain is the medium
the performer of climate

sigh shuts eyes
ear compasses
no east
no north
no anchor
no west
no south

in this percussive sea

droplets of condensed air
glass beads of thought

rain affirms
the serial propriety of the self

figure of dreams

*Images are not in the psyche as in a container but are the psyche.
In other words images mirror the psyche just as it is
– as constantly imagining.*

Robert Avens

the red lipstick girl
a figure of dreams says
it's my favorite colour
but it causes people to hurt me

the painful energy of the visible

the alien child
a figure of dreams says
do not be afraid
I am just mutating

the painful energy of differentiation

the front runner
a figure of dreams
says nothing
but beckons
me come

the painful energy of expectation

the architect
in a house of dreams
adjusts the blinds
and says
let me show you the Taj Mahal effect

the elusive trickery of light

the disciple
a figure of dreams says
you became my teacher
when you defeated me the first time

the liberating effect of defeat

the traveling companion
a figure of dreams says
we will go ahead
and meet you in a few days

left to follow
alone in a house of dreams
a Zen master says
abide where there is no abiding

up all night

> *We do not put the secret to sleep by dreaming of the impossible.*
> *On the contrary, the secret impassions the dream and the dream*
> *keeps us on the qui vive. "My God" keeps me up at night. The*
> *secret is first, last and constant.*
>
> *John D Caputo*

cry fire like you
really mean it
the mystic says

an exclamation
in excess of knowing

the great doubt
a dark night
can also be exclamatory

a terrible power
that obliterates
all certainty

then
the indiscretion
of insight

a kind of madness

an exclamation
in excess of knowing

keep us up all night
keep us up all night
the night
will keep us
in excess
of ourselves
unknowing

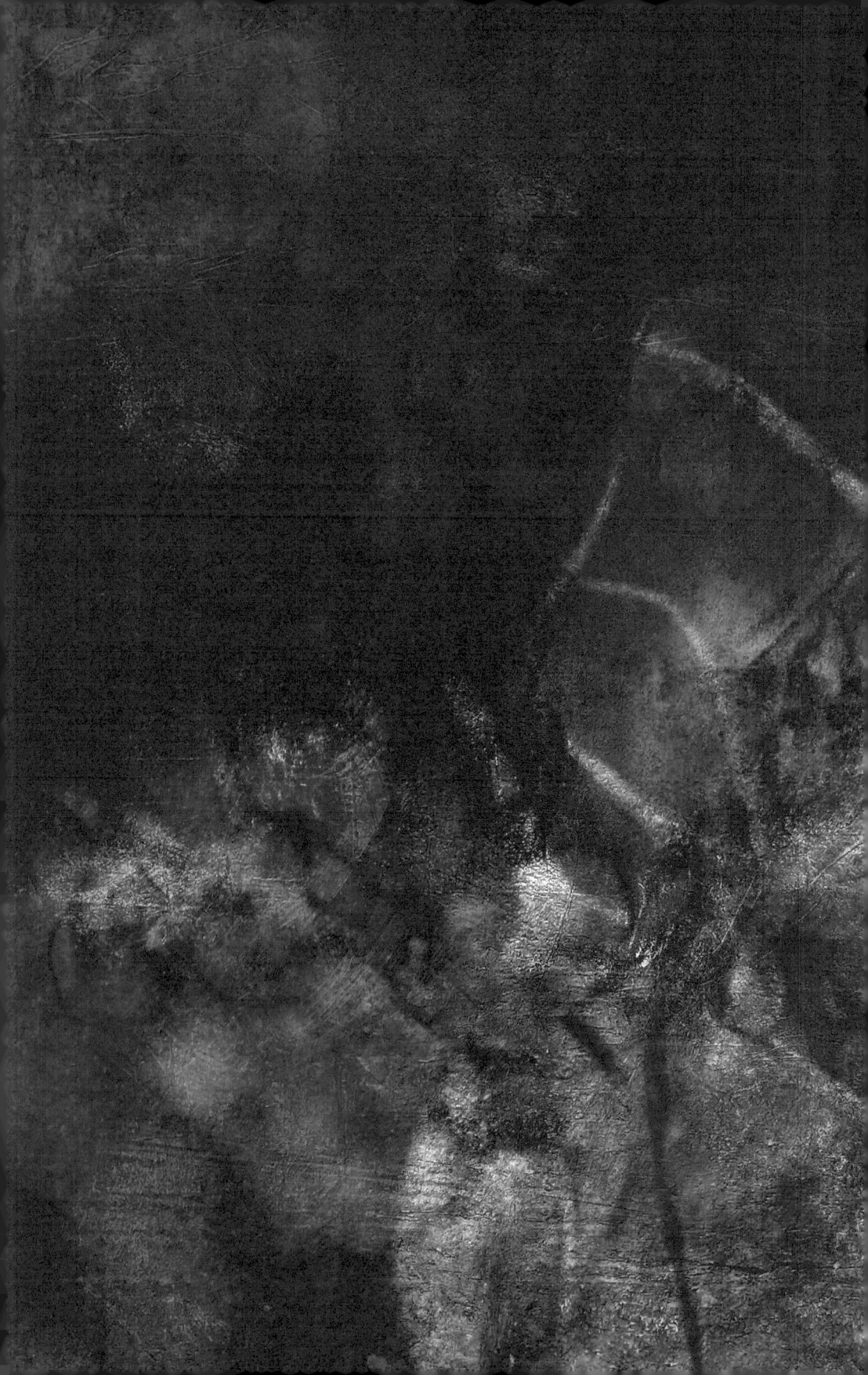

veil of tears

> *Deep down, deep down inside, the eye would be destined not to see but to weep. For at the very moment they veil sight tears would unveil what is proper to the eye.*
>
> *Jacques Derrida*

what can the eye see
when wet

this vision of tears
this weeping for which
we know not what

this knowing for
which we can
only weep

weeping and knowing
the eye congeals

insight becomes
a liquid salt

dried
a coarse dust
an abrasive
mineral intensity

taste what you cannot see

rubbed
let it scar you

don't look down
don't turn back
this viscosity
turns to rock

Four

art gallery Northampton Massachusetts

while pondering Jacob and his angel
        tiny figures
                barely visible in the
                        fierce scurry of paint

      I saw two boys
              stopped before the cases of antiquities

            one leaned
                  into the other's air
                        caressing without touch

on the canvas   not wrestling   yet
the other two   hold each other   lock step

walking   as questioning encounter
echoes   the grip of coming night

that   simple daily   gesturing of lovers

no need for combat no need for paralysing tricks of touch

            a look is a kiss
                        a kiss is a look
                        wet with longing.

getting ready

on the train
the boy covered in tats
including one where the
curve of the leg met the foot
which said
ready
the boy covered in tats
was drinking
coconut water
the woman in brown
pen paper phone
was making lists

on photographing black holes

i

I am in New York the weekend after
we have all seen the brightness of the dark sun
and we have suddenly······become
all seeing·······················at this event horizon
changed by······················this ring of data

·······························this ring of bright orange time

·······························something tricked into nothing
·······························nothing tricked into something again

·······························invisibility's sudden smile

ii

light to time passing

our eyes these·················white blossoms
bursting and···················soft with light

my days too····················have become eyes
hours lit from inside··········to gather
all that is there··············crisp and waiting

twisted························tangled imaginings
·······························an algorithm
decoded························for the first time

iii

Gershom Scholem said
the image escapes in every direction
his mystic cipher now
a shimmering fact even in
this vortex of disappearance

light to time passing

air tells of winter lingering

                        then suddenly space
                        opens dense with sun

touch me not

i

in this hour
light is dull
soundscape soft

spent day
has purchased
heart's strength

resonance
feeling's sketchy outline
hums imperceptibly

alone
body warmed
I nurse sorrow
incandescent
and holy

touch me not
do not weep

ii

Kristeva once called pain
philosophy's mute sister
she traced the explosion of
that frothy seed
(*a melancholia*)
whipped air and water
sea   wine   sperm

each a zero
each a sedating kiss
each a path to ecstasy

each an   opening
into   oblivion

she writes of
Dostoevsky
looking at Holbein
who said

there is nothing
more dismal than
this dead god

eyes' upper lid
closes to kiss
its lower half
and gently
sleep immerses

breath's thanks
is stopped

the body heavy with

life's mass
light with
soul's rising
lays prone
and silent

touch me not
do not weep

iii

I saw him   in the bushes
first light   last light
grief's darkness   no recognition
I held him
in my mouth
warmed
and licked him
with fierce
wet heat of
breath

I held him in my mouth

I held him
in my arse
hugged
and seduced him
with tight
moist grip
of spasming tissue

I held him in my arse

I held him
in the contorted
synapses of my mind
rocking him from side to side

I held him in my mouth
I held him in my arse
I held him in the contorted synapses of my mind
I lavished him with love
I lashed and scarred him

then he said   do not weep
then he said   touch me not

        as if death itself were a contagion
        as if resurrection were no antidote

I reach out and he is gone

*there is nothing
more dismal than
this dead god*

Five

Ariel's cycle

I am
and he the
hooded hunched stone weighed
my daemon   lover

also a sprite
green lithe phosphorescent
moons soft our night
landscape hilled and misty

the spiral
to air
climb
one   heave
two   sigh
three   stretch
four   not there   yet

more to turn and twist
to find   cut   embrace
the iced top winds
this blithe terrain
three peaks
three vales
daemon sprite lover

      ***

when dream
comes to
day's temple
image blisters
reality's sleek lines
find is fantasy
touch is air

head
feet led

and hand played
spins awry

open
open is
that slight hole
cavernous in
its intent

      ***

the beautiful curved
recess
stomach's pit
hollowed   empty
carved thrown or
blown like
fine Venetian glass
edge   razor fine
its line lacquered
by a rare translucent glaze

this ceramic container
my bleak sorrow

      ***

the boy
was naked
and laughed
as he
Ariel
climbed
the spirals
metal frame

impish and light
his steps
drawn thick
into the vortex

ascending
descending
energies

sex's cloak
creativity's frail bodice

        ***

the soul
is on trial
in this time

heart too

boundaries shattered
capillaries whipped
to frenzy

and you
who are soul's
companion
fidelity tested
to know
the real as image

        ***

I open this book
this red book
and write
to name

name
you
nothing is as
effervescent as a dream
no woodland sprite
capable
so many ruses

I open the book
to wet this page
to make mark
with blood
with blood
of image's
flesh

    ***

I am climbing
climbing
into your world
as you
climb
the tower's
metal rim

startled
a moment
caught hanging
hanging by
thread of sight
my laugh to yours
companionate
hearty
your eyes blue
pierced by
the density of
mine

    ***

I caught a glimpse of
Sylvia's substanceless blue
the eye's gaze narrowed
to perceive
such a palate of
nothing

the mix

so pure and bleak
it wrests the air
from blood's edge

      ***

head
cocked coy
and cheeky
androgynous but sharp

the figure
a boy's
but for the splash of hair
and the sallow
coloring
of the flesh's farthest
corners

a gentle shape
not yet
defined
not yet the wish
the will   to
impose itself
as set form
against world's
amorphous water

      ***

I will revisit
this place
in the flurry of
time's beckoning

the mischief of return
arm held out
eyes blinded
forefinger and thumb
clutching the donkey's tail

this piece
to be placed again
in finality   it seems
the thumbs tack
to pierce the right hole
and cover now
the chosen spot
with this year's
tangled mane of grace

        ***

and I saw
his eyes

I composed
on his tongue

a smile

A strange appearance: note on images

The images accompanying these poems are from an ongoing series: *A strange appearance – variations*. The series continues my engagement with abstracted variations on the landscape and still life traditions. In playing with these forms I seek to investigate our troublesome representation of 'nature': all at once beautiful, monstrous and mysterious.

What does it mean to call something strange? Or as ecological philosopher Timothy Morton frames it: how can anything not seem strange in a world that has been fundamentally altered at its core by the visible and invisible layers of human histories and human impact. If what we see is mere appearance and what is, is only partly apparent, then everything is very strange even when it doesn't appear to be.

Our world has been queered. Has in fact always been queer.

For Morton, the strange, the queer, the weird, present a kind of logic that balances knowing and not knowing, a new way of thinking more fitting for this world we find ourselves in.

The series explores this queered world, what Morton calls the "strange strangeness" of perception in the age of the Anthropocene. The layered, saturated imagery of my images evokes a sense of the 'dark-uncanny' which Morton postulates is a phase of 'dark ecology' as we pass from a 'dark-depressed' to a 'dark-sweet' more hopeful perspective.

Designed to evoke a sense of both outer and inner space, the images begin with close-focused photography of foliage, flowers and other elements of urban gardens. They are built up through digitally layering multiple images over painted textures from abstract cold wax paintings which in turn have been the result of obsessive layering. The process of construction and deconstruction inherent in this approach to image crafting, and the mix of digital and painterly aesthetics, makes explicit the persistent trace of the human hand in the 'natural' in our precarious times.

A strange appearance – variations takes one photogravure key plate developed through these techniques and then underlays a selection of different pigment prints to create variants which change in colour and form as the two layers intersect. This play with multiple variations speaks to both possibility and mutation: the open and the determined aspects of change. In an increasingly polarised world this play with the affiliation of shapes also signals the radical continuity as well as the rifts in similarity and difference.

Marcus O'Donnell, July 2024

Marcus O'Donnell is an artist, writer and academic. His fiction, journalism and poetry has been published in periodicals and anthologies including, *Verandah, Siglo, Bent Street, New Writing, OutRage, Hard,* and *The Conversation.* Marcus trained as an artist and exhibited in the 1990s and early 2000s but has only recently returned to public art-making after a time concentrating on his academic career.

In 2022 Marcus O'Donnell was awarded 2nd prize in the Jack Wilkins Experimental Photography Prize. He has been a finalist in the Milburn Landscape Prize (2023); the Mullins Conceptual Photography Prize (2023); the Olive Cotton Award (2023) and the Tacit Still Life Prize (2022). He is actively involved in the printmaking community and is a member of the Baldessin Press & Studio Committee of Management, a not-for-profit access, education and editioning studio. He is currently Provost at Navitas Careers and Industry, a private higher education provider.

www.ingramcontent.com/pod-product-compliance
Lightning Source LLC
Chambersburg PA
CBHW041806160426
43191CB00004B/66